The GREAT FIRE of LONDON

In 1666 London was already a big city. Half a million people lived there, and it had grown out beyond the old city walls.

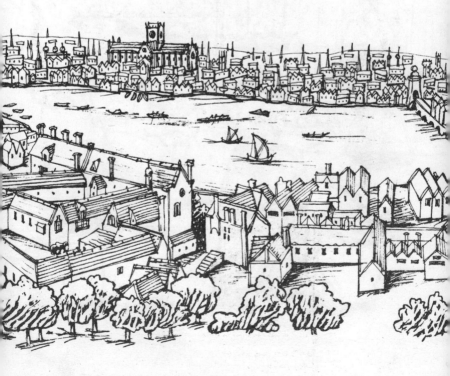

The summer of 1666 was very dry. Londoners were working as usual. But it was so hot, and the streets were filthy.

Tall wooden houses made the narrow lanes airless and dark. There was almost no room for the carts to pass through.

"Oi, look what you're doing!"
cried a raker. "We don't want the
Plague back this summer!"

He tried to sweep away sewage,
as people pushed by.

The year before, one hundred thousand Londoners had died of the plague. Rich people like King Charles II and the Lord Mayor had left London. They wanted clean air.

OXFORD
30 MILES

Saturday 1st September was another hot, dry day. In Seething Lane by the Tower of London, sat Mr Samuel Pepys, Clerk to the Navy.

Every day he wrote something in his diary – about his work, or life in London. Today he wrote about the danger of the drought.

"Everything is tinder-dry. The Thames is much too low. And there's a strong east wind too. Oh, dear." Pepys was worried. "I must speak to an astrologer," he decided. "I hope Mr. Lilly can tell me what will happen."

Few people were about that night. Robbers, known as footpads, hid in the shadows. Children holding lanterns led rich people safely home.

At midnight in Pudding Lane, the baker Thomas Farynor checked his ovens. Then he went upstairs and fell fast asleep.

Outside a warm east wind blew clouds of dust across the street.

Later the baker told his story.
"I woke up choking. It was two
o'clock. My maid was coughing
and there was smoke everywhere.
That's when I rushed outside... I
don't know where my maid is."

An hour later his house was
just smoke and ash.

The flames spread. First to the Star Inn, and then a gust of wind, and **Whoosh!** Sparks fell on the warehouses by the river. The pitch, oil and brandy in them made the flames worse. Thames Street was an inferno.

At his home in Gracechurch
Street, the Lord Mayor woke up.
He raised his head from the pillow.
"Pish! Only a small fire," he
yawned and went back to sleep.

Next morning, the east wind was still blowing fiercely. Three hundred houses had burned to the ground. A man shouted, "Fish Street Hill is all on fire!"

Pepys heard the news from his
maid. He hurried to the top of
the Tower of London to see for
himself. "Everything will burn,
even the churches! I must tell
the King!"

On the way to the Palace at Westminster, Pepys met a lot of angry people. Some thought God had sent the fire. Other people said foreigners living in London had started it.

Pepys just blamed dry weather and a foolish baker.

Pepys found the King at last and told him the dreadful news.

King Charles took command at once, and ordered, "First pull down houses in the fire's path. Then set up fire posts. My brother James will help."

Y ORDER OF THE KING

Make firebreaks.
Pull down houses
to stop the fire
spreading.

Set up fire posts.
Organise groups of
men to fight the
fire.

Get extra soldiers.
Call them in from
outside London.

Make waterpipes
from elm tree
trunks to help
carry water to the
fire.

19

But even a King could not
hold back a fire like this.
Flames soared thirty metres
into the city sky, and the
sun shone red like blood.

No one knew how to stop
the flames.

Some
people
say...

... you can
hear the fire
in Oxford!

21

"All we have here are fire buckets – and our church bells to warn people!

There's not enough water in the Thames to put the fire out!"

water pump

ladder

axes

leather fire bucket

hand pump

hook for pulling down thatch

The fires spread west and north. People stayed in their homes as long as they dared. At the very last moment they fled, in boats called wherries, or on foot.

Lucky carters made a big profit.

Pepys saw terrified pigeons die
because "they didn't want to
leave their houses. But my wife
and I will escape... And I'll come
back home tomorrow to bury my
wines and cheeses!"

It was Tuesday now, the third and worst day of the fire. All Cheapside's shops were ablaze. Ludgate Hill and Fleet Street

R. Fleet

Old Roman Wall

Chea

Fleet Street

St. Paul's

Wa

Ludgate Hill

Tham

N

RIVE

too. The fire was so hot that even the stones of old St. Paul's were burning.

"Flames are wading through the streets!" said the poet Dryden.

John Evelyn, who also kept a diary at that time, wrote that at night-time: "It was light as day for ten miles round about. Ten thousand houses all in one flame. Melted lead was running down the street."

That lead came from St. Paul's Cathedral. It fell from the roof when sparks lit the timbers. Wall stones exploded and even the pavements below were glowing with heat. The next day St. Paul's Cathedral was a ruin.

By the broken east wall, a
schoolboy called Thomas Taswell
saw a horrible sight – the body of
an old woman, "... her clothes
were burnt and every limb
reduced to coal."

Everyone was frightened. But the King rode straight to the fire, where he leaped from his horse to grab a firehook. With a quick tug he brought the burning roof thatch down, then he put it out with a bucket of water. People were happy to see their brave King.

Still the flames spread, north and west to Cripplegate and Fetter Lane.

It made Pepys sad to see the ruins. Hot ashes burned through

his shoes.

Near the smoking remains of the Royal Exchange he saw a shivering cat – all its fur burnt off, but still alive.

But then a
miracle happened.
The east wind
dropped.

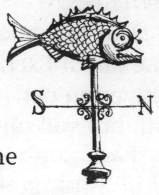

Now a breeze
blew gently from the
north. The fire had
come to an end.

Amazingly
only six people
had died.

The survivors huddled together
in Moorfields and Spitalfields.
Their sad little bundles held all
the belongings they could save
from the fire.

"Two hundred thousand people
of all ranks and degree in the
fields near the city..." wrote
Evelyn.

The King had to act. "We will have an Inquiry," he said. "First clear the rubble. Bring these people food and drink, and make them shelters."

Then he looked over the ruins.

LONDON on FIRE!
Four-fifths of City burnt
87 churches
13000 houses
44 Company Halls
St. Paul's Cathedral
The Guildhall
Royal Exchange
ALL DESTROYED!

There was a lot to talk about. How to stop more fires? How to rebuild London? But which first? No one could agree.

The King thought, "I want a
new, grand city. Build me one
like Paris!"

Clever Christopher Wren, the
new Surveyor of the King's
Buildings, was just the man to
grant Charles his wish.

Wren's London plan was excellent! It was every bit as grand as King Charles had hoped. But the King couldn't afford everything in it. He had spent all his money on a war against France.

In the end Christopher Wren built thirty-two new churches, each with a magnificent spire, and a great new domed St. Paul's Cathedral that was finished in 1711.

Every single new building had to be made of brick and stone, because wood burned too easily.

After the Fire there were other new 'Regulations' to follow.

The City set up fire brigades. People were careful to sweep up their rubbish. And, unlike the baker Thomas Farynor, everyone made their household ashes safe at night!

It took 10 years and more than seven million pounds to rebuild London. Today if you go to London, you might like to visit St. Paul's – or the Monument. Christopher Wren built that too, and it stands near Pudding Lane where the Great Fire began.

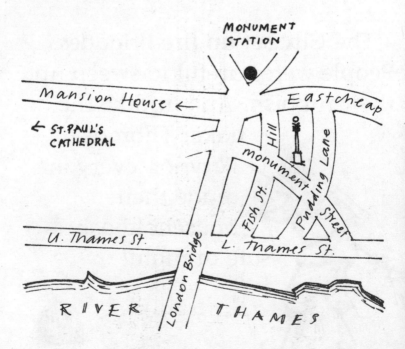

Timeline

1561   Old St. Paul's is struck by lightning. Timber spire burns away.

1603   Bubonic plague kills 30,000 people in London.

1616   William Shakespeare dies.

1632   Christopher Wren born.

1633   Samuel Pepys born.

1642   English Civil War begins.

1640   Charles I (Charles II's father) executed. The 'Commonwealth' begins under Oliver Cromwell.

1660   Pepys begins to keep his diary.

  The Restoration: England has a king again – King Charles II.

1661   John Evelyn attacks London's air pollution.

1665   Isaac Newton experiments on gravity.

  Summer: The Great Plague strikes London. Many people, including King Charles, leave the city.

1666   **February:** King Charles returns to London.

2nd-5th September: the Great Fire of London.

11th September: Wren presents his plans for rebuilding London.

25th September: Fire Inquiry begins.

1667   The Rebuilding Act sets out laws on how to rebuild London.

1669   Wren appointed surveyor of the King's Works. Pepys, worried about his eyesight, stops keeping his diary.

1675   Rebuilding of St. Paul's Cathedral begun.

1685   Charles II dies. His brother James II becomes king.

1686   Wren's 51 churches completed.

1689   James II replaced on the throne by his sister Mary and her husband, William of Orange.

1703   Samuel Pepys dies.

1711   St. Paul's Cathedral completed.

1723   Wren dies aged 91.

Glossary

all ranks and degree Every kind of person, including rich and poor.

astrologer A person who studies the stars and planets to try to see into the future.

Bills of Mortality Lists published each week in different areas of London saying who had died there and how.

diary A written record of daily events.

firehook A hook on the end of a long stick used to move burning material.

Inquiry A special investigation set up to find out why something has happened.

lead A type of metal, that used to be used a lot in the roofs and windows of buildings.

plague Deadly disease caught by humans from rat-fleas.

raker A street cleaner.

regulations Rules.

sewage Sludgy, dirty waste, mainly from baths and lavatories. Sewage used to be thrown out of houses into open channels in the street.